For my love Benjamin.
Your voice turned grief into
a weapon for change.
Your words taught us to
love and fight.

For Stephen.
Your memory taught us that love
must be stronger than hate.
Your spirits are forever linked in
the fight for a just world.

— Qian Zephaniah

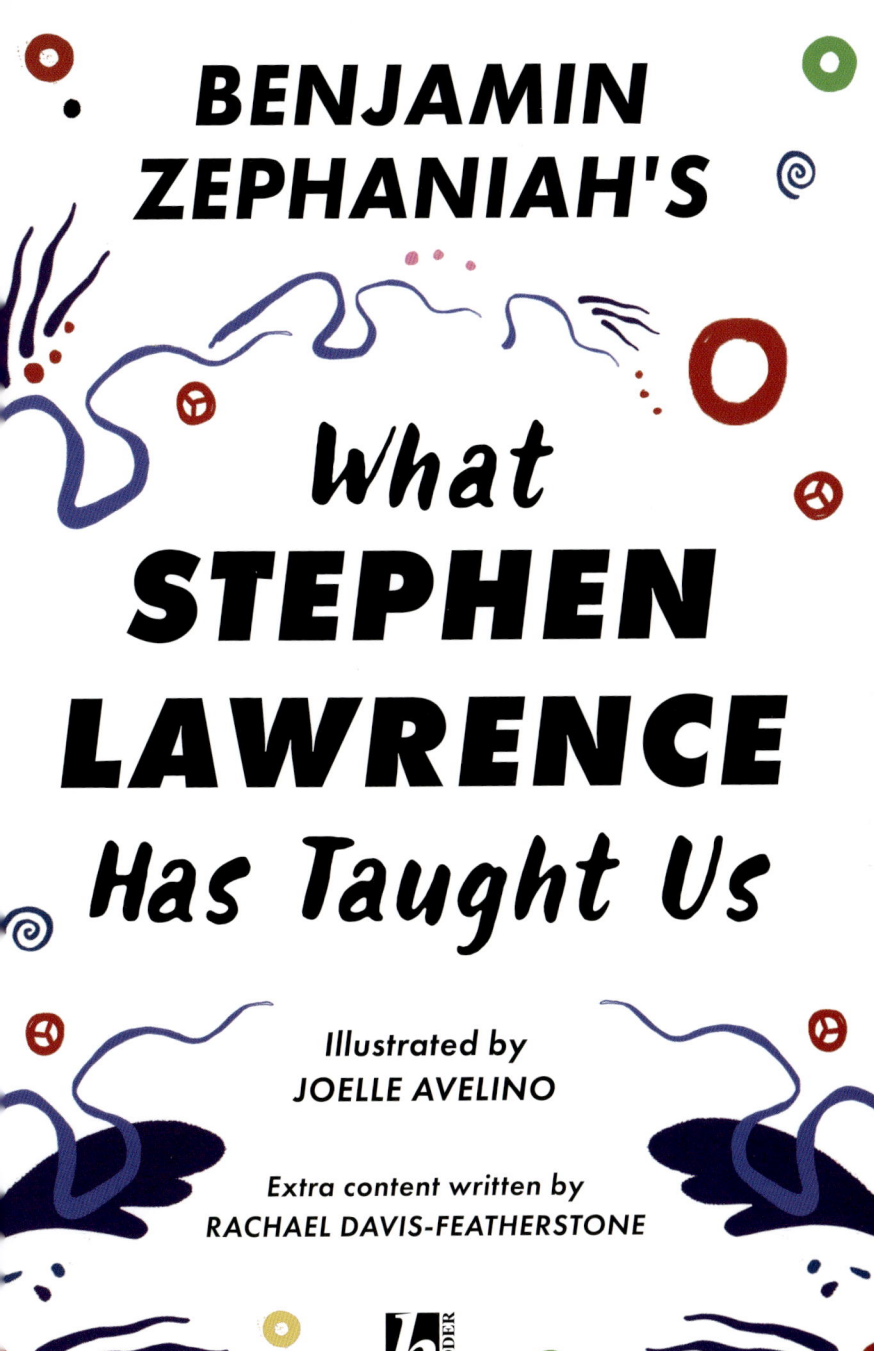

BENJAMIN ZEPHANIAH'S

What STEPHEN LAWRENCE Has Taught Us

Illustrated by
JOELLE AVELINO

Extra content written by
RACHAEL DAVIS-FEATHERSTONE

Hodder

Foreword

When I talk about my brother, I speak not only of the young man that he was, but also the man he was destined to become. Stephen dreamed of becoming an architect. He wanted to design spaces where people could live, learn and thrive. His life was full of promise, tragically cut short by an act of hatred that shocked the nation. Yet Stephen's story did not end there. From tragedy grew a powerful movement for justice, truth and change.

Benjamin Zephaniah was one of the voices who made sure my brother's name would never be forgotten. Although I never had the privilege of meeting him, I have long admired Benjamin and the principles he stood for – honesty, justice, equality and the unwavering courage to speak truth to power. Through his poetry and his sheer presence, Benjamin gave people hope and challenged us all to do better. That is why it is such an incredible honour that he chose to write this important poem.

Benjamin's words are fierce and uncompromising, yet also full of love. He reminds us that my brother's death must teach us to care for one another, to value every moment and to never turn away from the fight against racism.

For me personally, it is bittersweet: I never had the chance to thank Benjamin for taking the time to put pen to paper and share his thoughts and feelings around the loss of my brother. I wish I could have told him how proud I was that he decided to honour Stephen in this way.

My brother's legacy lives on through the tireless work of my family, through new laws and campaigns and through the young people who continue to believe in a better tomorrow. I hope Stephen's name stands as a reminder that racism must never be ignored, and that every voice raised for fairness and equality can make a difference to those who need it the most.

And so, as you read these words today, I want you to carry my brother's story with you. Let it remind you that your life has meaning, your dreams have value and your voice has power. My brother didn't get the chance to build the future he imagined – but each of you can. You are the architects of tomorrow. Build wisely, create bravely and do it all with love.

Hon. Dr Stuart Lawrence

What STEPHEN LAWRENCE Has Taught Us

Stephen Lawrence lived in South London with his family. In 1993, he was studying for his A-levels and wanted to become an architect. On the evening of 22nd April, while Stephen was waiting for a bus with his friend Duwayne, Stephen was involved in an unprovoked racist attack. He died from his injuries. The police knew who had attacked Stephen, but it would take nineteen years before any of the killers were brought to justice.

We know who the
KILLERS
are

As proud as sick Mussolinis, We have watched them
STRUT
before us

In 1994, Stephen's family launched a private prosecution but, frustratingly, charges against two of the accused were dropped before the trial, and in April 1996, the three remaining suspects were found not guilty due to a lack of evidence. At that time, the "Double Jeopardy" law meant no one could be prosecuted for the same crime twice. So Stephen's killers thought they had got away with murder. Feeling protected by the law, they flaunted their freedom on national television.

COMPASSIONLESS and ARROGANT

**They paraded before us,
Like angels of death
Protected by the law.**

It is now an open secret Black people do not have Chips on their shoulders,

Five years after Stephen's death, retired High Court judge Sir William Macpherson led an inquiry to investigate Stephen's case. The Macpherson Report found the police officers involved had been professionally incompetent, making multiple mistakes, and the police force had a culture of institutional racism. Now everyone knew the truth: the attack on Stephen was racially motivated and institutional racism had led to his killers not being brought to justice.

Benjamin Zephaniah, who wrote What Stephen Lawrence Has Taught Us, performed the poem on national television when the Macpherson Report was released in February 1999.

They just have **INJUSTICE** on their backs and **JUSTICE** on their minds.

Is as long as the road from SLAVERY

Liberty means being free to live your life without oppressive restrictions. The creation and enforcement of slavery took away Black people's liberty for generations. The UK government passed a law to abolish slavery in 1833 after a long and hard-fought battle. However, freedom from slavery did not guarantee Black people's liberty. The institutional racism demonstrated by the police force in Stephen's case is evidence that the fight for Black people's liberty was – and is – an ongoing battle.

The death of
STEPHEN LAWRENCE
Has taught us to
LOVE
each other
And never take the tedious task
Of waiting for a bus for granted.

After Stephen's death, his family wanted justice and to create a legacy for Stephen, so he would always be remembered. They wanted lessons to be learned from what happened to Stephen, and to make positive change to fight racism.

Watching his parents watching the COVER UP Begs the question

The Black community was outraged by the police not doing their job to serve and protect them. The Macpherson Report concluded that Stephen's killers might have been brought to justice if the police had done their job correctly in the first few hours after the attack.

What are the **TRADING STANDARDS** *here?*

Why are we paying for a **POLICE FORCE** *That will not work for us?*

In fact, Stephen might not have died. First aid was not given by the police who arrived at the scene. The police also made prejudiced assumptions about what had happened, and Stephen's friend, Duwayne, who witnessed the murder, was not taken seriously by the police. They then failed to collect vital evidence.

The death of
STEPHEN LAWRENCE
Has taught us
That we cannot let
the illusion of
FREEDOM
Endow us with a
false sense of security
as we walk the streets.

Stephen's killers continued to walk the streets as free men for nineteen years after murdering Stephen. That is two years longer than Stephen's entire life. Even today, this serves as a reminder that racism is not something of the past, it is sadly still prevalent in our world today.

The whole world can now watch the ACADEMICS and the SUPER COPS

The Macpherson Report was the first of many investigations into Stephen's case and the failings of the police involved. The findings described the culture of racism within the police force and offered recommendations, but the implementation of changes was slow.

Struggling to define
INSTITUTIONAL RACISM
As we continue to die in custody.

Meanwhile, many Black people were dying in police cells including Benjamin Zephaniah's cousin, Mikey Powell.

As we continue emptying
our pockets on the pavements,

And we continue
to ask ourselves
Why is it so official

That black people are so often KILLED without KILLERS?

Stephen was not the only Black person killed without the killers being brought to justice. There are many examples of murders of Black people that have not been acknowledged as racially motivated attacks and the killers have never been found or convicted.

*We are talking about
where we are now
We are talking about
how we live now
In dis state
Under dis flag*

*(GOD SAVE
THE QUEEN)*

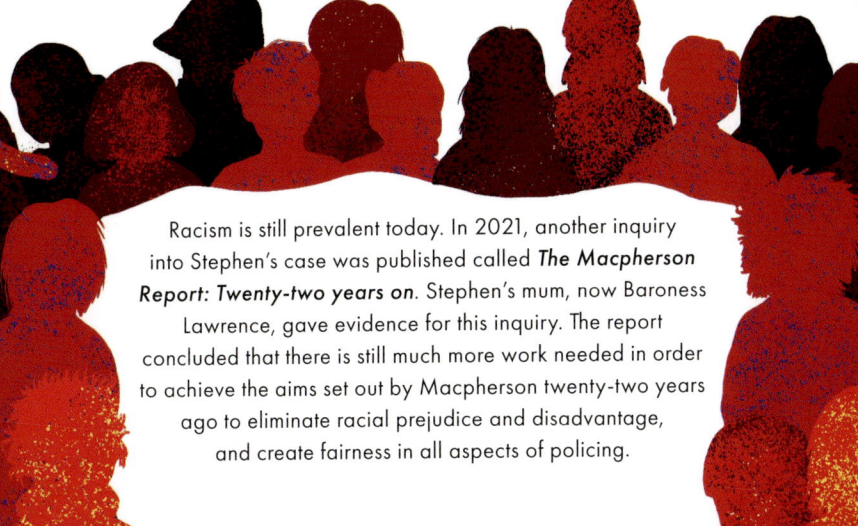

Racism is still prevalent today. In 2021, another inquiry into Stephen's case was published called *The Macpherson Report: Twenty-two years on*. Stephen's mum, now Baroness Lawrence, gave evidence for this inquiry. The report concluded that there is still much more work needed in order to achieve the aims set out by Macpherson twenty-two years ago to eliminate racial prejudice and disadvantage, and create fairness in all aspects of policing.

And God save all those black children who want to GROW UP

Stephen wanted to be an architect. In 1998, Stephen's parents, Doreen and Neville, founded the Stephen Lawrence Charitable Trust to help disadvantaged children achieve their dreams. Ten years later, the Stephen Lawrence Centre was opened to support this mission, close to where Stephen did his architect work experience.

And God save all the **BROTHERS** and **SISTERS** who like raving

Stephen loved hip hop and soul music, and he enjoyed going to concerts. His favourite artists were Leaders of the New School, Tupac Shakur, Ice Cube and Public Enemy.

Because the death of
STEPHEN LAWRENCE
Has taught us that
RACISM is **EASY** when
You have friends in high places
And friends in high places
Have no use whatsoever
when they are
NOT YOUR FRIENDS.

Having a friend with significant influence in politics or the media can help a person achieve their goals. This can be good and bad. For racists in the police force, having friends in high places meant protection. It meant they could behave in a way that wasn't right, without fear of reprimand. Still to this day, no criminal charges have been brought against the police officers involved in Stephen's case.

Thankfully, Stephen's family also had some friends in high places. When Nelson Mandela visited Stephen's family it increased the media attention on the case. Then, after Stephen's killers boasted about their freedom, the Daily Mail newspaper used its influence to be an ally to Stephen's family. The newspaper printed the faces of Stephen's killers on the front page under the heading: MURDERERS. This played an important role in getting the Macpherson Report commissioned. Without this, Stephen's killers might never have been brought to justice.

Paul Condon was the Metropolitan Police Commissioner when Stephen was murdered. In 1998 he publicly apologised for the police force's failings in bringing Stephen's racist murderers to justice. However, while he acknowledged that the police force had not done enough to combat racist crime, he refused to accept the police force was institutionally racist.

*Come to an honest place
And get some advice from your*
NEIGHBOURS.

*Be enlightened by our community,
Neglect your well-paid*
IGNORANCE

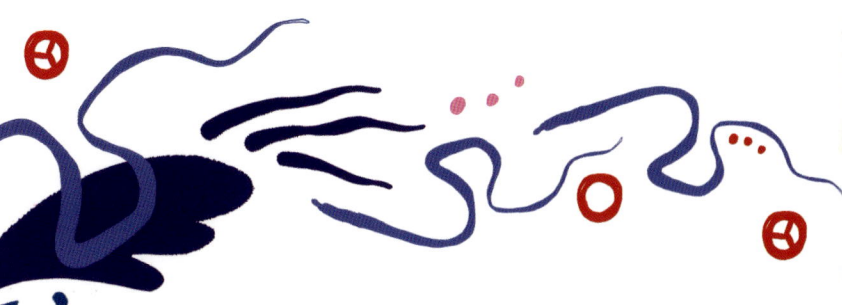

In 2014, an investigation concluded that the police force had spied on Stephen's family after his death to try to undermine the family's campaign for justice. Paul Condon said he knew nothing about this, despite being in charge of the police force at the time.

Stephen's family, the Black community and their allies continue to fight for Black people to be listened to and treated with respect and equality. In 2018, the Prime Minister announced that 22nd April would be a National Day of Remembrance, honouring Stephen. The Stephen Lawrence Day Foundation charity was set up in 2020.

Because **WE KNOW** who the **KILLERS** are.

Thirteen years after Benjamin Zephaniah wrote this poem, two of Stephen's killers, Gary Dobson and David Norris, were convicted of his murder. Finally Stephen had some justice. But for Stephen's family, it only felt like half-justice, as not all those involved in the murder were able to be prosecuted due to the failings of the police. However, we do know who the killers are. And more than that, through the tireless campaigning of Stephen's family, real change has been made to the law, police practice and attitudes to racism.

TIMELINE

13 Sept 1974
Stephen Lawrence is born (parents Doreen and Neville).

1988
Stephen runs the Greenwich mini marathon.

1991
Stephen does work experience for an architect.

6 May 1993
Stephen's family meet with Nelson Mandela. This creates media attention that gets the nation talking about Stephen's murder.

7 May – 23 June
The first arrests are made in connection with Stephen's murder.

18 June 1993
Stephen's funeral takes place. His body is later buried in Jamaica.

Apr 1996
The suspects are found "not guilty" due to a lack of evidence.

Feb 1997
The coroner's inquest finds that Stephen was "unlawfully killed by five white youths in an unprovoked racist attack".

14 Feb 1997
The Daily Mail prints the photographs of the five suspects on the front page of the newspaper with the headline "Murderers".

24 Feb 1999
Benjamin Zephaniah reads What Stephen Lawrence Has Taught Us on national television.

May 1999
The Home Office establishes the Lawrence Steering Group to implement recommendations from the Macpherson Report.

Nov 2000
The Race Relations Act is passed.

Sept 2010
New forensic analysis reveals evidence on Stephen's clothing.

Jan 2012
Gary Dobson and David Norris are convicted for Stephen's murder.

Mar 2014
The Mark Ellison Report concludes that the police spied on Stephen's family.

1992
Stephen begins studying his A levels: Technology, Physics and English Literature.

22 April 1993
Stephen is killed in an unprovoked racist attack at a bus stop in Eltham, London.

24 April 1993
A candlelit vigil is held for Stephen where he was murdered.

28 July 1993
The suspects are released without prosecution due to a lack of evidence.

Jun 1994
The Stephen Lawrence Campaign is started to raise funds for a private prosecution.

Sept 1994
Stephen's family launch a private prosecution against the five main suspects. This is the first ever private prosecution for a racially motivated attack.

Mar 1998
The judicial inquiry begins, led by retired High Court Judge Sir William Macpherson.

Jul 1998
Stephen's parents launch the Stephen Lawrence Charitable Trust.

24 Feb 1999
The Macpherson Report concludes the police force has a culture of institutional racism and makes seventy recommendations.

Apr 2005
The Double Jeopardy rule is abolished.

Jun 2006
Police open a cold case review into Stephen's murder using new forensic techniques that weren't around in 1993.

Feb 2008
The Stephen Lawrence Centre opens.

Apr 2019
The inaugural Stephen Lawrence Day takes place.

GLOSSARY

Ally
a person or group that has joined with
another for a certain purpose

Custody
kept in a cell by the police

Double jeopardy
a law that does not permit a person who has been acquitted or
convicted of an offence to be retried for that same offence
(this law was partially changed in England in 2003)

Fascism
a hateful, racist and oppressive political movement that
erodes democracy and freedom of speech

Home Office
the lead UK government department for crime, the police, drugs
policy, immigration and passports, and counter terrorism

Hypothetic
based on an idea rather than having roots in reality

Institutional racism
unequal treatment based on membership of a particular ethnic
group arising from attitudes and systems that have become
established within an organisation

Judicial
having to do with judges, law courts or their activities.

Macpherson Report, the
an important study in the UK that found the police had
problems with racism and gave recommendations to
make policing and society fairer and more equal

Mark Ellison Report, the
a study in the UK that showed the police made big mistakes in the Stephen Lawrence case and needed to be fairer and more honest

Mussolini
Benito Mussolini was an Italian dictator who inspired the growth of fascism

Nelson Mandela
a South African man who spent many years in jail fighting against unfair laws, and later became the country's first Black president, helping bring peace and equality to his people

Race Relations Act
a law made to stop people being treated unfairly or discriminated against because of their race or skin colour

Teletubby
a TV character with a screen on its tummy who loves to play

FURTHER RESOURCES

The Life of Stephen Lawrence
by Verna Allette Wilkins

Silence is Not An Option
by Stuart Lawrence

Growing Up Black in Britain
by Stuart Lawrence

Stephen Lawrence Day Foundation
https://stephenlawrenceday.org/

HODDER CHILDREN'S BOOKS
First published in Great Britain in 2026 by
Hodder and Stoughton Limited

Poem copyright © The Estate of Benjamin Zephaniah, 2026
Text copyright © Hodder and Stoughton, 2026
Illustrations copyright © Joelle Avelino, 2026
Foreword © Stuart Lawrence, 2026
Text by Rachael Davis-Featherstone

Benjamin Zephaniah *Too Black, Too Strong* (Bloodaxe Books, 2001)
Reproduced with permission of Bloodaxe Books.
www.bloodaxebooks.com
@bloodaxebooks (X/Facebook) #bloodaxebooks

The Estate of Benjamin Zephaniah and Joelle Avelino have asserted
their right under the Copyright, Designs and Patents Act 1988,
to be identified as the author and illustrator of this work.
All rights reserved. A CIP catalogue record for this
book is available from the British Library.

HB ISBN 978-1-444-98109-4
E-book ISBN 978-1-444-98110-0

1 3 5 7 9 10 8 6 4 2

Printed in China

Hodder Children's Books
An imprint of Hachette Children's Group
Part of Hodder and Stoughton Limited
Carmelite House, 50 Victoria Embankment, London, EC4Y 0DZ

An Hachette UK Company
www.hachette.co.uk
www.hachettechildrens.co.uk

The authorised representative in the EEA is
Hachette Ireland, 8 Castlecourt Centre, Dublin 15,
D15 XTP3, Ireland (email: info@hbgi.ie)

*The website addresses (URLs) included in this book were valid at the time
of going to press. However, it is possible that contents or addresses may have
changed since the publication of this book. No responsibility for any such
changes can be accepted by either the author or the publisher.*